Women Healing from Abuse

Women Healing from Abuse

Meditations for Finding Peace

Nicole Sotelo

Paulist Press
New York/Mahwah, N.J.

Cover design by Sharyn Banks
Book design by Lynn Else
Cover photo by Anton de Flon

Library of Congress Cataloging-in-Publication Data

Sotelo, Nicole.
    Women healing from abuse : meditations for finding peace / Nicole Sotelo.
        p. cm.
    Includes bibliographical references.
    ISBN 0-8091-4424-7 (alk. paper)
    1. Abused women—Religious life. 2. Abused women—Prayer-books and devotions—English. I. Title.
    BV4596.A2S68 2006
    242′.4—dc22

                                                                2006017740

Published by Paulist Press
997 Macarthur Boulevard
Mahwah, New Jersey 07430

www.paulistpress.com

Printed and bound in the
United States of America

I dedicate this book to my parents.

Contents

Meditations

CONTENTS

Acknowledgments

I am grateful for Nancy de Flon's prayers and support at Paulist Press. I also thank Nancy Richardson, Ilene Standford, Nancy Nienhuis, Laura Ruth Jarrett, Kerry Maloney, and my thesis seminar participants for their guidance, feedback, and nurturance of this project in its original form as my thesis. My gratitude also extends to all counselors, mentors, and friends who have helped my own healing journey. And, finally, deep thanks to the Spirit who helped bring me into being and who sustains this journey.

Introduction

Invocation

"Your faith has made you well; go in peace, and be healed…"
(Mark 5:34). Jesus speaks these words to a woman who sought
healing and who discovered that her faith could help her heal.
Perhaps you seek healing, too. You are not alone. For centuries,
women across the globe have suffered from abuse. Today it is
estimated that approximately one-third of women experience
some form of abuse—be it economic, emotional, physical,
and/or sexual—and many of these women seek deep healing
from the suffering that abuse causes. Millions of these women
are Christian and, like the woman in Mark's Gospel, seek healing from a spiritual source in addition to the healing typically
found in support groups, counseling centers, and shelters.

This book is for those of us who *do* seek a spiritual source
for our healing, just like the women of the Bible. It is for those
of us who have suffered abuse, know someone who has, or work
with those who have. It is a book for those who have experienced loss, loneliness, or disconnection from oneself, loved
ones, or community. As you begin using these meditations, I
pray that the Spirit will guide you on your healing journey.
May the Spirit guide us all away from a world where there is
violence, to a world of blessed peace.

The Healing Journey

As you begin your healing journey, you may wonder how this path will look or feel. The journey often begins well after any bruises have healed or any violent encounters have occurred. It may take weeks, months, or years before you feel ready to begin an active process of healing. A holistic healing journey will encompass your whole being—your physical, emotional, and spiritual selves. Unfortunately, in many healing settings, the spiritual self is left out of the healing process. Yet the spiritual self is often the most important aspect because it includes all parts of who you are in the deepest and widest ways.

By choosing to heal all parts of yourself—the physical, emotional, and spiritual—you have taken a courageous step. You have said "yes" to the healing journey, and you have said "yes" to making it a holistic process that includes all of your body, your mind, your heart, and so importantly, your spirit.

If you are just beginning to heal, it is often best that you seek the care of a professional counselor who will have the experience to help guide you safely along your path. (While healing, it is also important to remember that if you ever think about suicide, you call your counselor or check yourself into your local hospital at once.) You may also seek other people to help you heal, such as a pastoral worker, minister, friend, massage therapist, support group, or other person whom you trust and who has experience with women trauma survivors. If they don't have experience in this area, they may be able to refer you to someone who does. The National Domestic Violence Hotline may also refer you to local resources for safety and recovery. The appendix lists the contact information for this hotline and other sources for your healing journey.

The Three Phases of a Healing Journey

Once you have begun a healing journey, you may expect three phases on your path. These phases are marked by the need for safety, for remembrance and mourning, and for reconnection.[1] Nobody moves through these stages in neat, successive steps, but you will find yourself in each of these three phases at some point in your healing process.

The First Phase: Safety

The phase of safety is a critical phase for any woman's healing.[2] You must establish a safe environment for yourself, apart from the person who has abused you. If you have children, this includes creating a secure place for them as well. It is not an easy task, and you should feel free to call upon the support of family, friends, counselors, social workers, domestic violence shelters, and so forth. This phase of safety includes more than just physical distance from the person who has abused you. Creating a safe environment also includes developing healthy eating, sleeping, and exercising habits, and finding ways to support yourself and your family financially. Keeping yourself healthy and safe must also include the cessation of addictive or self-harming behaviors. This is the first step on your healing journey, and in order to proceed to future phases, it is critical that you begin to feel safe in your body and your environment.

Even once you have enacted these safety measures, you may still feel unsafe. It is common to feel fear, even after separating from the person who abused you. In fact, perpetrators of abuse may find and kill a woman after she has left. Thus your feelings of fear are not to be taken lightly. You may call upon a counselor, the police, legal aid, and/or a domestic-violence organization to help ensure your safety and the safety of any children you may have. Even when you are physically safe from the person who has abused you, you will probably still feel fear when memories surface or when your emotions are triggered by something that reminds you of the abuse. Thus it is essential during your healing process that you not only experience physical safety, but that you also seek emotional safety with the help of a counselor so that both your body and your heart find refuge.

Finally, in this initial stage of healing, you should also seek spiritual safety by seeking shelter *within* aspects of your faith that are healing, or seeking shelter *from* aspects of your faith that are harmful. Remember that physical or emotional abuse is also spiritual abuse. When someone mistreats your body or controls your emotions, this may also hurt your spiritual self since your spirit encompasses all that you are. Therefore, part of recovery from abuse includes recovery or renewal of one's spiritual self, particularly when the person who hurt you used scripture or religious attitudes to rationalize the abusive behavior, or when you felt that aspects of your faith kept you from seeking help.

You may find that seeking spiritual safety means taking shelter *from* aspects of your faith that do not aid your healing.

You may find that there are beliefs or practices in your religion to which you turned when you were in need that no longer seem life-giving. You may decide to seek shelter from some of these aspects for a temporary or long-term period of time. Some beliefs and practices that a number of women who have been abused find harmful include certain scripture passages, domineering language for God, theology that supports domination of one person over another, theology that valorizes violence and suffering, religious traditions that privilege male leaders or undermine women's potential, and so forth.[3] You may also feel that your relationship with God has changed as a result of the abuse or as an aspect of your healing. After experiencing abuse, it is not unusual to feel estranged from God or your faith community. You may wonder: Where was God or the people of your faith community during the moments of horror? Why didn't they protect you from the words or hands of the person who was hurting you? These are questions that you will likely seek to answer on your healing path. No matter what your answer may be, as you heal, it is important to remember that what happened occurred at the hands of the person who abused you and not by the will of God.[4] God does not desire us to suffer abuse. Instead, Jesus tells us that he walked the earth so that we "might have life, and have it abundantly" (John 10:10). A person who commits abuse disrespects and damages the abundant life that God intends for us. Some theologians who write on the topic believe that during abuse, God is still present with us.[5] God's presence remains when others have failed to stand with us, respect us, or protect us. The person who abuses someone may have turned away from God, but

God is always present to *you* as a source of healing and strength from which we may draw for our recovery.

It is with this understanding that many women have decided to remain within the Christian faith. They have discovered that, for them, seeking spiritual safety means taking refuge *within* some aspects of their faith. Just as you may feel that some aspects of faith are harmful to your healing journey, you may also find that there are aspects that will nourish you and provide you with counsel for your recovery. You may find comfort in scripture passages that speak about healing, in images of a loving and caring God, in liberation theology, or in the words of a well-trained, compassionate pastor. You may experience yourself growing closer to God than ever before as you walk the healing journey with God's support.

Each woman's path of spiritual safety is unique. Some women choose to leave their faith or religion behind due to painful memories or harmful beliefs and practices. Other women seek spiritual safety by entering more deeply into their faith or their own sense of the Divine. Many women do both—gathering around themselves the healing aspects of their faith and leaving behind or transforming the harmful aspects. Whatever you decide, just remember that God does not want us to suffer. God wants an abundant life for us. Our faith is not built on suffering but on our hope to move *beyond* the cross of suffering to a place of safety that will help us create a new, abundant life.

Reflection questions for safety:

- What do I need in order to create physical safety for myself and my children? Am I living in a safe house or shelter? Do I have my basic needs met, such as food, clothing, and health care?

- What do I need in order to create spiritual safety for myself and my children? How did the person who hurt me abuse my spirit and/or use my faith against me? Are there harmful beliefs or practices in my faith that I need to leave behind or find ways to reinterpret in light of what I have experienced? What are the life-giving and healing aspects of my faith from which I may draw during my recovery process?
- God wants me to be safe and I have a right to safety. Who can help me secure this safe environment?
- What do I need in order to create emotional safety for myself and my children? Do I have a counselor or support group who can help me at this time? Do I live in an environment where it is safe for me to express my emotions?

The Second Phase: Remembrance and Mourning

The second phase of healing is one of remembrance and mourning.[6] In this stage you remember and grieve your experience of abuse. This is not an easy task and should be done with the care of a professional counselor, along with any others with whom you choose to share your experience. Now that you have established a secure environment, you are more able to safely recall your experience of abuse at your own pace. Sharing your story will not erase the trauma you suffered, but you will be able to reflect on and integrate the experience into the whole of your life-story.[7] Abuse is overwhelming and it is easy for it to overshadow your entire life. During the healing process, it is not unusual to feel as if the abuse is the center of your life. But the second phase of healing helps you to recognize that although your experience will always be part of your life-story, it is not the only story in your life. As you progress in the phases of healing, the abuse will slowly find its place and you will emerge as the central figure of your life-story.

This second phase of healing takes place not only with your body and emotions but with your spirit. Spiritual remembering and mourning are important steps in this second phase. You may remember aspects of your faith that you felt were abusive or that hindered your healing in the past. You may also grieve the ways in which someone used your faith against you or broke your spirit during the experience of abuse. Remembering and mourning flow from the first phase of seeking spiritual safety, but this phase deepens the recollection of your own specific experiences. Did the person who abused you use the name of God during the cycle of abuse? If you were abused by your spouse, did a passage in the Bible tell you to submit? Did you think that you had to follow its direction even when that meant succumbing to abuse, rather than finding the love about which the passage speaks? Does your faith community look down upon couples that separate or divorce, and you felt you could not leave the relationship? Does your faith community admire and support the person who was abusing you and, therefore, does not believe your experience? Although this is a time for recalling and grieving the ways you were hurt, remember that grieving is not the end point. When you grieve, it is not because *you* have died, it is because you have experienced a loss or a hurt. Mourning helps you to heal from loss, harm, or hurt and to prepare for the abundant life ahead of you.

Reflection questions for remembrance:

- What are some stories that I can remember from my experience of abuse? Who will help me to remember these stories in safety? (If you need a counselor, please see the appendix for the National Domestic Violence Hotline and a list of counseling organizations that may refer you to a counselor in your area.)
- What is the saddest part of the abuse I experienced or witnessed? What have I missed in life because I was caught in a cycle of abuse?
- What particular experiences of abuse harmed my spirit? Are there aspects of my faith that were used against me or that hindered my ability to seek help — explicitly or subtly?

The Third Phase: Reconnection

Finally, the third phase of healing is one of reconnection.[8] Now that you have shared and mourned your story of abuse, you feel more capable of inhabiting and living out the rest of your life-story. You begin to imagine a future for yourself, a future that includes the presence of healthy relationships with family, friends, coworkers, or a faith community. You no longer feel that the experience of abuse completely overwhelms you, but rather that you have survived and are ready to experience the world once again. You may find yourself more capable of connecting with and trusting others, whether people from your past or new people. You may also come to recognize that your suffering is part of a pattern of suffering by women across religions and societies. This recognition may prompt you to take up a "survivor mission" and work for an end to violence.[9] Having experienced abuse and healing, you may seek ways individually or with an organization to ease the suffering of others or to seek to prevent violence from occurring in the future.

This third phase, like the others, has a spiritual aspect, too. After you have created a safe environment and remembered and mourned the abuse you experienced, you may choose to reconnect to your faith anew and share your new faith perspectives with others. You may find new meaning within Christian scripture, tradition, or your own faith community that gives support to your healing path. Before, for example, you may have found it difficult to connect with the figure of Jesus if you experienced abuse at the hands of a male, or if the person who abused you used your faith against you. In this third phase, perhaps you begin to see the figure of Christ through a new, healing perspective. Jesus may become a model of someone who tries to counter violence and act for right relationship. Jesus does not abuse women, but rather meets women where they are suffering and offers to assist them in their healing, as witnessed in many scripture stories. You may discover the figure of Christ and others in your faith life that offer a model of relationship that does not include abuse but, rather, respectful and peaceful connection.

Therefore, as mentioned before, this final phase is one of reconnection—with your body, emotions, *and* spirit. Here, the various stories of your life come together into a single story—your *story*. And, most of all, you feel more whole. Your body, emotions, and spirit feel united again in one, abundant, precious life—yours.

Reflection questions for reconnection:

- Do I have dreams for myself with which I wish to reconnect? Dreams of education or a particular career? Dreams of a healthy, loving relationship or family? Dreams of changing aspects of my religion or society so that there is less violence and suffering?
- Who are the people from my past with whom I wish to reconnect? Are they people who will support the healing I am doing and will respect all of me—body, mind, heart, and spirit? Do I want to begin meeting new people? How will I ensure my safety in these new situations as I begin to trust again?
- Are there aspects of my faith with which I want to reconnect? What aspects of my faith do I want to hold onto that will help my new life to flourish? Do I want to remain in or reconnect with a faith community? How do I relate to the Divine now?

Preparing for Your Healing Journey

This book is created so that you may come to experience the power of prayer and begin to pray in a way that will help you to heal physically, emotionally, and spiritually. There are countless, creative ways in which God's grace will assist you in your healing journey. Everyone's healing path takes different roads and everyone prays toward their healing in unique ways. Use the following suggestions to map your own path.

Making It Your Own Journey

To begin, you may choose to incorporate the meditations of this book into a daily prayer practice. A daily practice enables you to connect with a healing, spiritual source each day. Monks keep a daily rhythm of prayer so as to have a recurring reminder of their connection with the Divine and to make of their lives a living prayer. You, too, may choose to incorporate a daily rhythm of prayerful healing into your day to set the foundation for your holistic recovery.

Find a time of day for prayer that is most appropriate for you. Some people elect to pray in the morning when their bodies are still rested or when others in the house may be asleep. Others opt to pray midday as a way to break from their busy schedule for a moment of renewal. Finally, others may choose to pray in the evening as a way to rest their bodies after a long day. Contemplate what times of your day could benefit the most from some life-giving prayer.

Once you dedicate a time of day, you may choose the length of your prayer time, lengthening or limiting parts of the meditation. Generally, you may expect to spend at least ten or fifteen minutes in prayer, with more time allotted if you choose to do one of the activities that follow each meditation.

Now that you have a time in mind, you also may want to create a place in your home where you may pray safely and without interruption. When choosing an area, ensure that it is a place that feels comfortable and protected to you. You may find that a corner of your bedroom is the perfect place, or perhaps there is a special place in your garden where you can sit undisturbed by family or friends. Take a walk around your living space and find the spot that is right for you. If the place where you are living does not feel like a safe place to pray, you may decide that a bench in a local park, a pew at a church, or a place at work is more suitable. Think about the places open to you that feel comfortable and safe.

Once you have found a place, if it is one that you may decorate, you may want to adorn the space with an altar or images that will call you to a peaceful mode of prayer. Imagine the different places in your life that have been sacred to you, and remember the elements in that space that have drawn your attention. Was it a Catholic church with an image of Jesus or Mary? Or perhaps you recall a Protestant church with large windows full of sunlight? Maybe your memory is that of a quiet setting in the desert or woods or at the ocean. How might you set up an altar or area of your home with objects that draw you to the sacred and remind you of these or other holy spaces? Perhaps you love the ocean and will choose to place some shells on a table next to a picture of a loved one. Or you may wish to arrange some rocks from a walk in your neighborhood on a shelf near an open window to welcome fresh breezes. Take a few moments to allow your imagination to fly freely and then decide what you will bring to your sacred space.

Once you have created your prayer area, you may choose how to begin and/or end each meditation. Some women choose to light a candle or make a sacred gesture. You may also begin each meditation with a few moments of relaxation exercises so as to calm your mind, body, and spirit in preparation for prayer or in transition to the rest of your day. As a woman who has experienced abuse, your body may be in "alert" mode most of the time. You have become accustomed to being attentive to the slightest sound of agitation and the accompanying fear of being hurt. As a way to calm yourself and to become more fully open to experiencing the healing presence of God, centering and relaxation techniques help profoundly.

One simple relaxation practice is that of "breath awareness." Sit upright in a chair or on the floor. Feel the ground beneath you, supporting your body. Become aware of your back and spine holding you upright. Move your shoulders back into alignment so that your chest is lifted and your heart feels open. Feel how your heavy head is held strongly by your neck. Become aware of your breathing—in and out, in and out. Feel your breath moving in through your nostrils. Imagine the cleansing air filling your lungs and flowing into every limb of your body, healing every cell that has been hurt. This air is the healing, life-giving gift of the Creator. Spend a few moments just watching the miracle of your breath and body, nourishing you, sustaining you, and bringing you to awareness of the Spirit within and around you.

Another easy relaxation technique is a "senses alive" exercise. Begin this one like the one above by sitting and becoming aware of your breath. As each breath comes in, imagine it traveling down into your lungs and moving out through each part of your body. Every part of your body that receives the oxygen receives new life and energy: your head, neck, shoulders, arms, hands, chest, abdomen, legs, and feet. Imagine that as the air passes through each part of your body, it brings the sacred breath of new life. It awakens that part of your body to the day. You may choose to raise your hands and arms or feet and legs one by one. Try wiggling them as you may have done as a child, silly and wild. Then, let them rest again. Feel the energy pulsing in them. Take a few moments to relish the feeling of being restfully alive.

Once you learn these techniques, you may use them to begin and/or end your prayer sessions. You may also choose to use these techniques during the day when you feel over-whelmed or need a moment of rest.

On Your Way

When you are ready to begin praying, there are two ways to approach the daily meditations. You may decide to follow them day by day as compiled in a linear fashion, one for each day of the week for a series of four weeks. Then, you may use them month after month as you walk your healing path. Alternatively, you may choose to use the book by picking a different medita-tion each day according to the themes listed in the Contents that correspond with the type of healing you need that day; for exam-ple, if you are feeling particularly fearful one day, you may choose the meditation entitled "Safety." If you are feeling lonely, you may pray the meditation entitled "Friends." The three stages of healing and their characteristics have been incorporated into the daily meditation themes. Thus, as you move through the meditations, you will recognize the stages of recovery and be able to reflect upon the changes in your own healing.

The format of the meditations follows a simple outline of a scripture passage, scriptural reflection, personal quiet time, prayer, and response. To begin, read silently or aloud the scripture passage and reflection. Then take a few minutes to sit quietly. You may reflect on the reflection question(s) or simply sit in silence. If you use the reflection questions, you may choose to ponder them in your heart or to write or draw your feelings in a journal. Afterwards, read the concluding prayer. Feel free to add your own words of prayer to those that are written or create your own. Finally, there is a response section. This section includes a list of ways to incorporate the healing theme of the meditation into your day. These suggestions offer you the opportunity for your whole body to *respond* to the meditation so as to pray holistically and live the healing theme of the day. Each meditation has three suggestions; choose one according to your place on your healing journey. The first suggested response will always be one that may be done quite simply and individually for the days when you feel overwhelmed by your trauma. The second suggested response invites more active engagement with the day's theme. Finally, the third suggested response enables you to stretch your healing and often interact with others as a way to connect your recovery more tangibly with the world around you. Whatever level of activity you choose to do, it is your personal response and will assist you in turning your daily prayer for healing into a healed life.

In the prayers, I have included ways of naming God that have helped me on my own journey of healing. As you pray, you may use these names or other names that you know for God that help you to connect with the Divine in a healing way, perhaps with innovative language and fresh images. For example, before beginning your healing, you may have feared God and thought of God as a judgmental, all-powerful being who could punish you for wrongdoing. Perhaps now you find yourself angry with God. Instead of hiding in fear, you decide to share your feelings of anger with God. Perhaps now you choose to connect to God as the Loving Companion on your healing journey. You will find that as you heal, your relationship to God, yourself, and the world will change—including the way that you call upon and relate to God the Divine.

Lastly, you may note that this book uses the words *we* and *us* at times. In writing this introduction and the spiritual reflections, I have intentionally used the words *we* and *us* when describing the experience of women who have suffered abuse. I do so because all women, at some point in their lives, have experienced oppression and/or abuse and its subsequent suffering. Without dismissing the gravity and specificity of the violence endured by women who have been beaten, raped, tortured, or murdered, I want to emphasize by this choice of words how universal violence is against women, all women, despite ability, age, class, ethnicity, sexual orientation, religious affiliation, or no religious affiliation. By using the plural pronoun, I also aim to underscore the necessity of our subsequent solidarity with one another. We all need healing and we all need to support one another along that path.

Blessing for Your Journey

This is the end of the introduction and the beginning of your healing journey in prayer. I ask the Spirit to be your gentle guide. I pray that this book will be a compass on your path, with the true north always pointing in the direction of your holy healing. May your healing strengthen you and the world in which we live. I offer daily my prayers for and with you.

Meditations

Week One

Safety

...The doors of the house where the disciples had met were locked...Jesus came and stood among them and said, "Peace be with you." (John 20:19)

Reflection: After the crucifixion, the disciples were scared that they may be hurt as Jesus was. They ran to a shelter where they could lock the doors and console one another. Nobody could get in to harm them. The disciples were finally safe. The only one to enter their sanctuary was Christ, who brought them the gift of peace. As women who have experienced and witnessed suffering, we need to find safe space like the disciples. We need to be in the company of those who will comfort and protect us. We need to be in a place where we can finally greet peace.

Am I in a safe space now? Where do I feel peace? Is there somewhere I may go to feel safe? Who are the people who will help me to secure safety and peace?

(Pause for quiet reflection.)

Prayer: God, my Refuge, sometimes I feel afraid and unsafe. At times, I know that I am at risk and that I need to find safety.

At other times, I know that I am safe, but my heart still remembers those times when I felt vulnerable. You helped lead the disciples to shelter and to company that would comfort them. Now, I pray you will assist me in finding a safe space for my body, emotions, and spirit. Help me to find protection. Help me to know your peace.

Response:

1. Safety is the most important step in your healing journey. Without safety, it is difficult to set in motion the healing process. To begin, you may want to try this simple affirmation: "I want to be safe. I have a right to safety." Say this phrase ten times in the morning as you wake and ten times before you sleep. Watch how your relationship to safety changes.

2. It helps to remember moments from your past or in your daily life when you felt/feel safe and to ask those experiences to help you understand what you need to feel secure. Ask yourself, "When have I felt safe?" Is it a physical space? Is it a space in your mind? Then ask yourself, "How does that safe space feel?" Notice what you are able to do in that space when you feel secure.

3. This week, pay attention to your feelings of safety. When do you feel comfortable? What is there in common about the places where you feel comfortable? Do you feel more comfortable when you are out of the house or in the house? Are you comfortable with coworkers or friends? Is there someone who can help you create new safe spaces?[1]

My Body

God saw everything that [he] had made, and indeed,
it was very good. (Gen 1:31)

Reflection: When we have been hurt by abuse, it affects our
bodies for a long time. The harsh words may stop and the
bruises may heal, but our bodies remember the physical, emotional, and spiritual pain. Sometimes it is difficult to feel our
own emotions or think our own thoughts because the person
who hurt us tried to keep us from being an individual. At other
times, emotions seem scary because they bring painful memories. When we do feel emotions, they may be negative ones
directed at ourselves. Perhaps we feel ugly or ashamed because
we were told that we were not beautiful. And yet, God invites
us to live in the beautiful bodies that we were given, full of mar-
velous emotions and thoughts. Our bodies were created to be
loved, not to be abused. God wants our bodies to be whole
again so that we might spend our lives knowing that we are
made in the image of God, and that we are very good.

How may I care for my body today?

(Pause for quiet reflection.)

Prayer: Creator God, in the beginning you formed me in your
image, blessed me, and told me I am good. But someone has
taken my body for granted. Someone has not seen the holiness
that resides in me. Someone has told me that I am bad. But you

have told me the truth. You have told me that I am created in your sacred likeness. Help me to remember that my body was beautifully made by you and that I am safe in my body. Help me to look in the mirror today and say, "Indeed, I am very good."

Response:

1. Today, when you look in a mirror or see yourself in a window's reflection, say, "I am created by God. I am beautiful and good."
2. Wrap your arms around your body and give yourself a hug. Tell your body, "I remember you. You are welcome in this world."
3. Go for a walk where you feel safe. Feel the ground beneath your feet as you walk on the holy earth. Remember that you are part of this sacred creation.

Memories

When the sabbath was over, Mary Magdalene, and Mary the mother of James, and Salome bought spices, so that they might go and anoint him. And very early on the first day of the week, when the sun had risen, they went to the tomb....As they entered the tomb, they saw a young man, dressed in a white robe, sitting on the right side; and they were alarmed. But he said to them, "Do not be alarmed; you are looking for Jesus of Nazareth, who was cru-

cified. He has been raised; he is not here. Look,
there is the place they laid him. But go, tell his disciples and Peter that he is going ahead of you to
Galilee; there you will see him, just as he told you."
So they went out and fled from the tomb, for terror
and amazement had seized them; and they said
nothing to anyone, for they were afraid.

(Mark 16:1–2, 5–8)

Reflection: The women who stood at the foot of the cross witnessed the violent death of Jesus. They traveled to his tomb to
anoint his body according to Jewish custom; however, when
they arrived at the tomb, they were met by a young man. He
shared with them the news that Jesus had risen from death!
The young man asked the women to share this good news with
the disciples and to return to Galilee. The women were frightened, but we know from other scripture stories that these three
women found the courage to move through their painful memories of the crucifixion and to follow Christ to new life. Today,
as women who experienced and/or witnessed violent abuse, we
are like the women at the tomb. We hold memories of abuse
and we may feel frightened at the road ahead of us. But the
three women at the tomb who were messengers of new life to
the disciples are messengers to us, as well. They announce that,
beyond the tomb of our memories and the fear we experience,
we may choose the path of life!

The three women at the tomb were fresh with memories
of the violence they had witnessed at Jesus' crucifixion, but

they announce to us that there will be new days beyond us if we follow the path of life.

Who are three women or men in my life with whom I may stand or to whom I may turn when I am fresh with memories of abuse but do not want to remain with those memories?

(Pause for quiet reflection.)

Prayer: Comforting God, sometimes I witness something and it reminds me of the abuse I suffered. Sometimes a loud noise or the shout of someone on the street triggers feelings of fear. I want to run away. I want to curl into a ball. When this happens, help me to remember that I am safe or help me to find a place and the company of people where I may feel safe. Help me to know that I am not trapped in the tomb of my past memories but that I may rise to new life!

Response:

1. When something in the present triggers a memory of something from your past experience of abuse, it is important to regain a sense of safety. Seek a place where you feel secure. Say to yourself, "My name is _____. I am safe."[2]

2. To root yourself in the present, try this rainstorm exercise that will bring your focus to the present moment. Sit comfortably in a chair with both of your feet on the floor. Begin by holding your hands in front of your chest and rubbing them together as if you were cold. Notice how it sounds like the beginning of a gentle rain.

Increase the "rain" by snapping your fingers. First one, then the other. Increase the speed until it sounds like the rapid fall of raindrops. Then pat your thighs, one then the other, with increasing speed so that the raindrops sound heavier. Begin stomping your feet at the same time to create a heavy downpour. Do this for a few moments. Then let the storm "pass" by settling your feet back on the floor. Next, stop patting your thighs and go back to simply snapping your fingers. Finally, end the storm by rubbing your hands together and slowly let the storm pass away. Sit for a few moments and feel the sensations in your body, alive to the present.[3]

3. If you feel comfortable, try doing exercise 2 with a friend or group.

God

My God, my God, why have you forsaken me?
>   Why are you so far from helping me, from the
>   words of my groaning?
O my God, I cry by day, but you do not answer;
>   and by night, but find no rest. (Ps 22:1–2)

Reflection: "My God, my God, why have you forsaken me?" These words are not only from the psalmist, but are also spoken by Jesus on the cross. Why do people suffer? Where is God amid the suffering? Where was God when we were suffering from emotional, physical, and/or sexual abuse? There are no simple answers. Sometimes there is only silence. We cry by day and no relief is found. We sob by night and no release is offered. Could it be there is no God? Or does God cry, too? God, are you crying with us? If so, come closer when you cry. Come cry *with* us, God. Come closer....come closer. Let us see your face. May we not cry alone.

God, come close to me and let me know you are near.

(Pause for quiet reflection.)

Prayer: God, where are you? Do you see my tears? Did you see how I suffered? Did you see my bruises? Did you see my blood? This is *my* body. This is *my* blood. I, too, have been broken. Have I, too, been forsaken? I am waiting, God. I am waiting. Come quickly. Come now. My God, my God, do not forsake me.

Response:

1. Where was God when you were suffering? Perhaps you could ask God. Take a few moments to ask God: Where were you when I was suffering? Where are you now? Now listen, and hear what message arises in your heart in response to your questions.
2. You may find comfort in speaking with a friend about your doubts. Often other people have doubted God's existence and assistance during a period of suffering— whether abuse, illness, or the death of a loved one. If you feel comfortable, ask a friend if she or he has ever felt abandoned by God and share your own feelings of doubt or abandonment.

3. Sometimes it helps to talk with a chaplain, pastoral counselor, or spiritual director about your faith journey during this time of suffering and healing. If you feel that you would like to explore your relationship with God with someone like this, there are many professionals available through churches, pastoral counseling centers, or retreat centers. Some may even specialize in helping those who have suffered abuse. Try calling a few and let your heart guide you to the one with whom you feel most comfortable. Remember that *you* are interviewing them in a sense. You are under no obligation to choose anyone if you're not comfortable. Check the appendix for a listing. You may also be part of a faith community and feel comfortable talking with your own minister, priest, or religious sister.

Giving Up

So Abraham rose early in the morning, and took bread and a skin of water, and gave it to Hagar, putting it on her shoulder, along with the child, and sent her away. And she departed, and wandered about in the wilderness of Beer-sheba.

When the water in the skin was gone, she cast the child under one of the bushes. Then she went and sat down opposite him a good way off, about the distance of a bowshot; for she said, "Do not let me look on the death of the child." And as she sat opposite

him, she lifted up her voice and wept. And God heard the voice of the boy; and the angel of God called to Hagar from heaven, and said to her, "What troubles you, Hagar? Do not be afraid; for God has heard the voice of the boy where he is. Come, lift up the boy and hold him fast with your hand, for I will make a great nation of him." Then God opened her eyes and she saw a well of water. She went, and filled the skin with water, and gave the boy a drink.
(Genesis 21:14–19)

Reflection: Hagar is separated from her home and abandoned by the father of her child. She wanders in the desert, unsure of her next meal, unsure of the direction of her life. Everything in life has been taken from her. As she runs out of water, she also runs out of her thirst for life. She held on to the last drop but even that is gone now. The only moisture that remains is the tear forming in her eye, and even that drops away from her.

In the middle of this dry land, God calls to Hagar. God encourages her not to give up on life but to open her eyes again, to give life another try. She opens her eyes to see her surroundings in a new way and discovers a well of life-giving water.

As women who have suffered abuse, there are days when we thirst for healing and yet our energy for life has run dry. We feel as though we can't take another step. We feel as though we can't even take care of the people and things we love the most. But in this story, God reminds us that we don't have to be afraid of these days. Instead, God calls us to keep opening our eyes to find the things and people in life that will nourish us with life-giving water—for the sake of those we love, for the sake of ourselves.

Sometimes giving up seems like the only option, but there are people who depend on me for life and there are people on whom I can depend, too. *Who depends on me like Hagar's child? On whom may I depend to help me open my eyes to the nourishing wells in life?*

(Pause for quiet reflection.)

Prayer: Living God, there are days when I feel like Hagar and want to give up. My life has run dry and I have nothing left to live for. Help me to open my eyes like Hagar. Help me to see things in a new way—from the beautiful shades of gray in a cloudy sky to the beating of my heart that promises to keep me alive.[4] Help me to draw the nourishing water from life's deep and plentiful well. Quench my parched life and bring me back to life again.

Response:

1. You are alive. During the abuse, you thought that you might not live, but you did. During the pain, you thought that you might have to give up, but you didn't. Something within you decided to choose life over death. There is a part of you that wants to live. Let that part of you speak. What does she say? Why did she want to keep living? Let her cry her message to you. Let her sing her message to you. Let her live.

2. List or draw the different people or passions in your life that keep you excited to be alive. Do you have a friend who makes you laugh every time you are together? Do you wait every year for the beauty of autumn foliage? Think of everything from the most mundane to the most magnificent.

3. After being abused and surviving, it may feel as though you are living in a different world. Go out and explore your new world. Look around you and see what is beautiful in this world. Listen and hear the glorious sounds. Touch the textures of this world. Taste something sweet. Relish the colors and brilliance of this new world.

Self-Blame

Now he was teaching in one of the synagogues on the sabbath. And just then there appeared a woman with a spirit that had crippled her for eighteen years. She was bent over and was quite unable to stand up straight. When Jesus saw her, he called her over and said, "Woman, you are set free from your ailment." When he laid his hands on her, immediately she stood up straight and began praising God. But the leader of the synagogue, indignant because Jesus had cured on the sabbath, kept saying to the crowd, "There are six days on which work ought to be done; come on those days and be cured, and not on the

Sabbath day." But the Lord answered him and said, "You hypocrites! Does not each of you on the sabbath untie his ox or his donkey from the manger, and lead it away to give it water? And ought not this woman, a daughter of Abraham whom Satan bound for eighteen long years, be set free from this bondage on the sabbath day?" When he said this, all his opponents were put to shame; and the entire crowd was rejoicing at all the wonderful things that he was doing. (Luke 13:10–17)

Reflection: After an experience of abuse, it is difficult to rejoice. We may feel unworthy to rejoice, heal, or love. We may even blame ourselves for the abuse we experienced. We think, "If only I had acted differently or said something else, then the other person would not have reacted the way he or she did." But this biblical passage does not focus on why the woman was bent, or what she might or might not have done, or what might have been done to her. Instead it reminds us that everyone deserves healing, always. The religious leaders in the passage, perhaps like the self-blaming voices in our head, give Jesus a reason for why the woman should not heal: "She could have done this; she should have done that." But Jesus disagrees. Both he and the woman with the bent back know that all creatures of God are worthy of healing whenever we are in pain. All of us deserve healing that will help us to stand upright and be free!

What voices, from my head or from people in my life, tell me that I should suffer? Is there another voice within me or from someone I know that tells me I should deserve to stand upright and be free?

(Pause for quiet reflection.)

Prayer: God of Right Judgment, I sometimes feel that if I had done something differently, I would not have been hurt. I feel that this situation is my fault. But then I remember Christ's actions in this biblical story. He does not blame the woman for the pain she feels. Instead, he gets frustrated with the voices that keep her from healing. Help me to surround myself with people whose voices will support my healing rather than blame me for the abuse I suffered. Help me to remove the blaming voices in my head so that I, like the woman in the story, may heal and stand up straight. Help me to transform those voices into a new, affirming voice that will proclaim, "Woman, you are set free!"

Response:

1. It may be difficult to feel your own self-worth after being told, explicitly or implicitly, that you are the cause of all problems. You may feel a lot of self-blame about the pain you have endured. But you are not the cause of any abuse. There is never any reason for someone to verbally, physically, and/or sexually hurt another human being. Even though you may *know* this, it may be difficult to *feel* this. Try challenging the self-blaming voices in your mind. When you find yourself thinking, "Maybe if I was…" or, "Perhaps if I

had been…," give those voices a new phrase. You may try saying silently or aloud, "I am God's special creation and I deserve to heal," "I am worthy of a truly loving relationship," or another sentence that affirms you and the healing you deserve.

2. You may feel bent, like the woman from the biblical passage, burdened by lingering self-blame and other effects of a hurtful encounter. You may ache to stand upright and on your own. Try this meditative exercise. Sit on the floor with your ankles and feet tucked underneath your buttocks, as if you were kneeling and then sat down on your legs. Then lay your chest over your knees so that you find yourself resting in a fetal position or "child's pose." Imagine the negative inner and external voices of self-blame like rocks on your back. Feel the weight of the stones. Can you name some of them? What do they feel like? How does it feel to be bent over? Now imagine positive voices of self-worth to be light piercing the stones. Perhaps the stones break and crumble, or perhaps the light softens the stones. Feel the burdens on your back becoming lighter. Now imagine the light embracing you and filling your lungs and limbs with levity. Begin to feel the tingling as your body awakens. Slowly begin to move your fingers and toes. What does it feel like to be able to move again? Gently straighten your back and head into an upright position. Then begin to move your arms and legs and gradually rise. Feel the light lifting your body. Feel its warmth emanating from within you and all around

you. How does it feel to stand again? How does it feel to be free?

3. It may be difficult to feel worthy of positive relationships with other people or God. One way to practice confirming your own self-worth is to allow yourself to receive first the world's affirmations of you. If you walk outside today, feel the earth's gratitude for your presence on its soil. If it is raining, feel the sky's blessings on your shoulders. If it is sunny, sense the rays' delightful dance on your face. Before you fall asleep, imagine the moon anointing your body for its night of rest. If you encounter someone who compliments you, receive the affirmation into your heart.

Self-Care

Now as they went on their way, he entered a certain village, where a woman named Martha welcomed him into her home. She had a sister named Mary, who sat at the Lord's feet and listened to what he was saying. But Martha was distracted by her many tasks; so she came to him and asked, "Lord, do you not care that my sister has left me to do all the work by myself? Tell her then to help me." But the Lord answered her, "Martha, Martha, you are worried and distracted by many things; there is need of only one thing. Mary has chosen the better part, which will not be taken away from her." (Luke 10:38–42)

Reflection: Work may be a way to temporarily forget the memories of abuse. Work is also necessary to support you and your children. For a variety of reasons, women recovering from abuse often must work long hours each week and rarely have time to care for themselves. In this passage, Jesus reminds us to take time for ourselves. We may take care of ourselves in different ways: a full night of sleep, a morning prayer, a healthy lunch, a few deep breaths while waiting at a red light or waiting for public transportation, a game of soccer, a phone call to a friend, an evening walk. In caring for ourselves, we are better able to heal and better able to work. In caring for ourselves, we are able to spend some time during our busy day with ourselves, with friends, and with God—and that is choosing the better part.

What is one thing I can do today to care for myself?

(Pause for quiet reflection.)

Prayer: God, I haven't always taken care of myself. I was taught that I should care for others. But today I am reminded that you want me to care for myself, too. I am reminded that it is good to love myself just as you love me. Help me to find a few moments today when I can put aside one of my many tasks and just sit with you as Mary did. Help me to care for myself and love myself again. Love for myself is something that nobody can take away from me.

Response:

    1. Instead of jumping out of bed when the alarm goes off, take a few moments just to breath fully and slowly.

Imagine this pace of breathing setting the pace for your day: deep, slow, and steady.

2. You may have many demands on your time from people whom you love, including children, partners, friends, and extended family. Do not be afraid to ask for time off. Ask a friend to take care of your children for the evening and then return the favor another evening for her or him. Ask your partner to assist with household chores if you normally do the majority of the housework. You deserve free time. You are a woman who constantly cares for others. You deserve to have others care for you, too.

3. Sometimes it seems impossible to rest amidst a great deal of activity. If you are able, take some time off from your daily schedule. What is possible? An extended lunch break? An afternoon off? A long walk in the evening? A weekend away on retreat or vacation? Any time will help to renew your spirit.

Week Two

Home

How lovely is your dwelling place,
  O LORD of hosts!
My soul longs, indeed it faints
  for the courts of the LORD;
My heart and my flesh sing for joy
  to the living God.

Even the sparrow finds a home,
  and the swallow a nest for herself...

(Ps 84:1–3)

Reflection: Home has not always been a lovely dwelling place. It is often a place of mixed emotions where memories of pleasure rub roughly against memories of pain. Sometimes we still feel unsafe or scared in our living space even though the person who caused us pain may no longer be present. The image of the person who hurt us may still be fresh in our minds and influence the way we feel and act in the place we now call home. As we move forward in our healing, we often seek a new place to call home where we may feel free to be ourselves. We seek a new place where our hearts and flesh may sing for joy to the living God.

When have I felt at peace in a home setting? What made it feel so peaceful and comfortable?

(Pause for quiet reflection.)

Prayer: God, a home is supposed to be a place where I am unafraid to be myself. I have not felt a real sense of home for a long time. Help me to create a new feeling of home where I live now. Ease the hurtful memories and create a space within my heart for a new sense of home to be built. The psalm says, "Even a sparrow finds a home." Guide me as I find a nest for myself.

Response:

1. Each time you walk through the threshold of the place that you call home right now, bless the space. Create a simple blessing that you will remember and may speak silently or aloud. You may choose to say something like "Bless my home" or "May I feel free here."

2. Imagine someone you love dearly. Perhaps she or he is a friend or a family member or an image of God. Imagine standing at the entrance to the space that you call home right now. Imagine taking the hand of the person or image you have chosen. How does it feel? Are you happy? Comforted? Excited? If you feel secure with this person or image, imagine yourself entering the place that you call home with the person at your

side. Walk through each room of the space. Together, bless each room with warmth, love, and peace.

3. Whether you are living in an apartment, a house, or a temporary shelter, you may still create a home for yourself and family. Write a list of things you would like in a home space—not just physical characteristics but also environmental qualities. For example, you may want a physical space that is just yours where you feel comfortable, such as your bed or sleeping area. Your new sense of home may also include an environmental quality that gives you peace of mind and heart, such as a no-shouting rule or a request for a moment of silence before meals. As you write the list of attributes that you would like in your living space, let your heart dream as widely as possible. This week choose one item from your list to make a reality and begin creating your new sense of home.

Children

Now every year his parents went to Jerusalem for the festival of the Passover. And when he was twelve years old, they went up as usual for the festival. When the festival was ended and they started to return, the boy Jesus stayed behind in Jerusalem, but his parents did not know it. Assuming that he was in the group of travelers, they went a day's journey. Then they started to look for him among their relatives and friends. When they did not find him, they returned to Jerusalem to search for him. After three days they found him in the temple, sitting among the teachers, listening to them and asking them questions. And all who heard him were amazed at his understanding and his answers. When his parents saw him they were astonished; and his mother said to him, "Child, why have you treated us like this? Look, your father and I have been searching for you in great anxiety." He said to them, "Why were you searching for me? Did you not know that I must be in my Father's house?" But they did not understand what he said to them. Then he went down with them and came to Nazareth, and was obedient to them. His mother treasured all these things in her heart. (Luke 2:41–51)

Reflection: In this story, Jesus' family is celebrating the feast of the Passover, the festival of liberation from abuse at the hands of the Egyptian Pharaohs. You and your children may also feel liberated from abuse, but you may still worry about your children's welfare. As we search for our own healing, we may also be searching to reconnect with our children, as Jesus' parents were. Will my children ever heal from the abuse? Will my children and I ever feel like a family again? The biblical passage reassures us. The parents of Jesus had a "community of travelers" who would protect and care for their child, just as today we know that we may receive help in raising our children, from our community, whether it is family, friends, neighbors, counselors, teachers, or ministers. The scripture passage also reminds us that not only did Mary and Joseph have a community of travelers to care for their child, but they also had God to watch over their child. They find Jesus safely in the house of God. God is always with our children. This is something that we, as mothers, may treasure in our hearts.

What words or actions may I share with my children today to remind them that they are always under great love and care?

(Pause for quiet reflection.)

Prayer: Divine Parent, I feel overwhelmed. It takes so much energy to care for my healing and myself. I worry sometimes that I don't have the capacity to care for my children, too. Will my children and I ever find healing? I feel liberated from the abuse, but I know we have not crossed into the Promised Land. Light our path, O God. Give us a community of travelers with whom we may walk. Grace my children with your constant love and protection. Be parent to my child. Be companion to me. Let us be family again.

Response:

1. Sometimes abuse brings us numbness and silence. It may be difficult to feel your own emotions, let alone express deep loving emotions with your children. Or perhaps you never had a model of how to raise children in a healthy, loving environment. Despite this, what loving emotions might you share with your chil-

43

dren today? A story about their younger years that will make you both laugh? A long hug? A caring look into their eyes? The words *I love you*?

2. It is difficult to take care of children when you are hurting. You wish that someone could take care of *you*. Imagine ways in which you may care for your children *and* yourself. Can you make a nutritious meal for you and your children? Can you put them to sleep right at their bedtime so that you have some extra hours for yourself? Can you call their favorite relative or family friend to take care of them while you take some much needed time off?

3. As you move into a new way of being family, possibly without the presence of the person who was hurting you and/or your children, you may want to begin using new, healthy ways of relating to your children. What might you do to make this a reality? Think about your own upbringing. Are there certain caring and loving behaviors you learned from your own parent(s) or other people's parents? If you did not have models of loving behavior, you may choose to recall some of the unloving behaviors that you witnessed and reflect on alternatives to those. You may also think about the people and families you know today. Are there ways that they love one another that you would like to model with your own children? Do they eat meals together? Do they talk without shouting? Do they forbid the use of negative language against one another? Make a list of new behaviors and parenting skills that you like and incor-

porate one into your family each week. You may want to list your new rules someplace in the house where your children may see them and be reminded of these loving ways of living.

Age

Now Abraham and Sarah were old, advanced in age; it had ceased to be with Sarah after the manner of women. So Sarah laughed to herself, saying, "After I have grown old, and my husband is old, shall I have pleasure?" The LORD said to Abraham, "Why did Sarah laugh, and say, 'Shall I indeed bear a child, now that I am old?' Is anything too wonderful for the Lord? At the set time I will return to you, in due season, and Sarah shall have a son"....

Sarah conceived and bore Abraham a son in his old age....Now Sarah said, "God has brought laughter for me; everyone who hears will laugh with me." And she said, "Who would ever have said to Abraham that Sarah would nurse children? Yet I have borne him a son in his old age."

(Gen 18:11–14; 21:2, 6–7)

Reflection: Sarah laughs to think that anything new might happen in her life. "I have grown old," she says. "Shall I have pleasure?" She laughs in disbelief. But miracles happen. She gives birth to a son. And this miracle brings the laughter of joy again to her life.

As women moving away from abuse, we may feel as though healing will never come. Will we ever laugh again? We are too old, too busy, too poor, too hurt. We laugh to think of ever having enough time, enough peace, enough money, and enough pleasure. But seasons change. Each season brings a new seed, a new harvest. And in due season, we who are healing will give birth to something new. We, too, will laugh with true joy again.

What would I like for my healing harvest to yield?

(Pause for quiet reflection.)

Prayer: God of All Ages, there are so many barriers to my healing. I fear that I don't have enough time or resources in my life to make significant changes or to make progress in my healing. But you are a God who brings to birth new life in every age. Be with me from age to age, from my memories of youth to my dreams of the future. May I give birth to a new season in my life. May Sarah and I laugh together.

Response:

1. It may be difficult to imagine giving birth to something new in your life right now. What do you wish could be brought into your life to aid in your healing? Draw a picture of what you would like to see emerge.
2. Imagine you are a child again. Take a pen and paper and write a letter to your adult self with your less dom-

inant hand (that is, if you are right-handed, write with your left hand, and vice versa). What does your inner child say to you now? What wisdom does she have for you? Now switch the pen to your dominant hand and write a letter from your adult self to your inner child. What do you say in response to her? What news and laughter do you wish to share with her?[1]

3. It is easy to be scared to try something new, but you can start with small things. Try a new recipe. Write a poem or love letter to yourself. Go dancing. Attend a sports game, maybe one that features women players. Sign up for a class at your local university or education center. Be creative. Give birth to something new!

Dreams

If you sit down, you will not be afraid;
> when you lie down, your sleep will be sweet.

(Prov 3:24)

Reflection: When we survive abuse, we may feel as if we will never sleep peacefully again. We may suffer from troubling dreams. Sometimes the dreams are vivid retellings of the violence we experienced. Sometimes the dreams are new stories that leave us feeling scared. And sometimes the dreams are scenes of beauty that at last give us hope for our healing.

Do I recall my dreams? Is there a dream I remember from my childhood or from a recent night of sleep? How did I feel in the dream? Did the dream hold a message for me?

(Pause for quiet reflection.)

Prayer: Gentle God, sometimes I have trouble sleeping because my dreams leave me feeling frightened. At other times, just the mere presence of darkness scares me. The nights are long. Morning comes, but sometimes the dreams linger in the shadows of my day. When I wake from these dreams, remind me to touch my feet to the floor and my hands to the light so I may distinguish past darkness from present light. Open my eyes to realize that the nightmares are not my dreams. Open my heart to recognize that my dreams will once more be the hopes I have for healing, the visions I have for justice, the dreams I have for life.

Response:

1. Remember a dream that you enjoyed, or create a dream that you wish you had. Before you go to bed, recall this dream. What was the setting? Was there someone else in the dream? What did you like most about the dream? Savor this image and let it rock you to sleep.
2. Keep a dream journal. Each morning write down your dreams. You may feel the dream has a message for you and you decide to take the message with you into the day. Or perhaps you had a nightmare. Use the journal as a way to remove the frightening image from your mind and close it in the journal. If you don't remember your dreams, try writing your own dream!

3. Sometimes we want to share a dream. Is there some-one special in your life—a counselor, a coworker, a family member, or a friend—with whom you want to share this dream? Find a safe time and place to share your dream. Ask if they have a dream to share with you.

Trust

"The kingdom of heaven is like yeast that a woman took and mixed in with three measures of flour until all of it was leavened." (Matt 13:33)

Reflection: The woman in this story takes a small handful of yeast and stirs it into her bread dough. Nothing happens. But in time, she discovers that the yeast has given rise to enough dough for multiple loaves of bread.

As women who are healing, we have lost trust—in our-selves and in other people. As we begin to trust again, it is important to be gentle with ourselves. It is important to take a small handful of feelings or a little story from our life and share it with someone with whom we feel comfortable. We may be tempted to tell everything or we may not want to share any-thing at all. But, like the woman in the Gospel, stir in a little yeast and dare to wait. In time, you may discover this was just the right amount. In time, you will be given an abundance of bread that nourishes your life. To trust others and ourselves again, we have to take a risk—but only a small handful at a time. And then wait for the trust to rise.

Is there someone in my life, perhaps an old friend or coworker, with whom I may share a small handful of my life?

(Pause for quiet reflection.)

Prayer: God, I have lost most of my trust in myself and in other people. I may have also lost my trust in you. Where were you when I needed you most? Where were my friends? Where was my family? I still do not know the answers to these questions. But I do have faith that somewhere in this world, there is someone who will trust me and someone I can trust. Perhaps it is someone who is already close to me. Perhaps the person I can begin to trust again first is myself. Today, I will add a small handful of trust to my own heart.

And then I will wait.

May it rise.

Response:

1. After surviving abuse, it may be difficult to trust yourself. Try thinking or speaking this meditation in your bedroom, bathroom, or some safe space before leaving your home: "I trust my feet to carry me through today. I trust my heart to keep beating today. I trust myself today."

2. Think back to yesterday. What was something you did where you trusted yourself? Did you share your own opinion with someone? Were you able to draw upon your own inner knowledge to carry out a task at work? What might you do today?

3. Is there someone in your life—a coworker, a family member, or a friend—with whom you feel comfortable? If so, you may want to share something from your life with them. Remember, you don't have to tell them something that is emotionally painful. You may start by talking about a book you recently read, a current news event you saw on television, or a good recipe you tried for dinner. As time goes on, you may share more of yourself and find that they share more of themselves, too.

Advocating for Yourself

From there he set out and went away to the region of Tyre. He entered a house and did not want anyone to know he was there. Yet he could not escape notice, but a woman whose little daughter had an unclean spirit immediately heard about him, and she came and bowed down at his feet. Now the woman was a Gentile, of Syrophoenician origin. She begged him to cast the demon out of her daughter. He said to her, "Let the children be fed first, for it is not fair to take the children's food and throw it to the dogs." But she answered him, "Sir, even the dogs under the table eat the children's crumbs." Then he said to her, "For saying that, you may go— the demon has left your daughter." So she went home, found the child lying on the bed, and the demon gone. (Mark 7:24–30)

WOMEN HEALING FROM ABUSE

Reflection: This woman knows that she is her own best advocate. She has to be. She has to advocate for herself and her daughter because nobody else knows what is exactly best for them. So she enters the room where Jesus is resting and tells him what she needs. At first he says he must minister to the Jews first, and then as much as says that the Gentiles are considered to be dogs in their society. But the woman knows that she is human just like Jesus and that all people deserve healing, including her daughter. The woman tells him how she feels, and then Jesus heals her daughter. Her daughter is healed because the woman—against all customs and habits—knew her needs, used her voice, and spoke her truth.

Has there been a time in my life when I spoke up for what I believed or needed?

(Pause for quiet reflection.)

Prayer: All-Knowing God, the Syrophoenician woman knew what she needed. I don't always know what *I* need, but I do know I need healing right now. So like the woman in the Gospel, I also ask you for healing. I ask you to help me be the best advocate for myself: to discern what I feel and to speak up for what I need. Help me to create another miracle. Help me to know that *I* am the miracle and that I am worth advocating for.

Response:

1. It may be difficult to discern your feelings. Sometimes you are full of emotions. Other times you feel numb. Take a few moments to sit quietly. Ask your body to

share a feeling with you. What is that feeling? Does it have a name such as anger, fear, frustration, joy, relief, or sadness? Try saying the name of that feeling out loud. "I feel_____." Thank your body for sharing this feeling.

2. Sometimes words do not come for feelings but your body shares the feelings in other ways. Try letting your body share its feelings in a new way. Paint your feelings, dance your feelings, play your feelings, cry your feelings.

3. As you get in touch with your feelings and needs, you may want to try sharing them. You may be in a situation where you don't have a choice so you have to start speaking for yourself or your children even when you aren't sure exactly what you need. Go ahead. Try speaking what you feel. Try advocating for what you need. If you are being abused by your domestic partner, do you need to ask the police for a restraining order or to call a domestic violence hotline to ask about openings? If you are healing from parental abuse, do you need to know about availability of low-cost counseling? Remember, you are your best advocate!

Telling Your Story

And a woman in the city...having learned that he was eating in the Pharisee's house, brought an alabaster jar of ointment. She stood behind him at

his feet, weeping, and began to bathe his feet with her
tears and to dry them with her hair. (Luke 7:37–38)

Reflection: The woman who bathes Jesus' feet tells the story of
her trauma with her tears. She wipes away the pain with her
hair. She weeps in gratitude for the healing that has begun.
Sometimes it is difficult to find words for what you have experienced. Sometimes the pain is so great that it is difficult to speak.
During these times, our tears tell our story. During these times,
it is fine to just cry—alone or with someone else. It is fine not to
share everything. It is fine to take your time. So when you feel
safe and want to share your story, let it pour out of you—in whis-
pers, in song, in dance, in color, in silence, in tears.

*Do I want to share my story with someone? Is it safe for me
to share my story? How will I share my story?*

(Pause for quiet reflection.)

Prayer: God, I want to share my story. After so many years of
silence, I must speak. But sometimes when I try to speak, I cannot. Sometimes I can only cry. You welcomed the woman in the
scripture passage to speak through her tears. Help me also to find
a safe space and safe people so that when I am ready, I might tell
my story in a way that I feel comfortable with. I know you are
with me when I tell my story. I know you are with me when I cry.

Response:

1. If you feel you want to tell your story, you may want to
   start by telling it to yourself. You needn't recall it all at

once. You may simply want to close your eyes, remember an image or a word for one moment, and then open your eyes again.

2. If you want to share a little more of your story with yourself, you may want to say a few words, draw a picture, or sing, dance, or pray your story in a place that feels safe. Telling your story isn't about writing a documentary of your past from start to finish, including every little detail. Telling your story is about finding a safe place to share remembered moments that were significant to you, and about knowing that you may stop sharing those moments any time you choose.

3. If you feel comfortable sharing your story with someone else, is there someone in particular with whom you want to talk? Who feels safe? Who will honor your story? Is there a counselor at the local hospital, health center, or church? You may share your story with friends or family, too, but it is important to have someone who has been trained in helping survivors of trauma to guide you through your story-sharing. You may even find it helpful simply to sit with a counselor who will let you cry in a safe space before you decide to share your story. Remember that you don't have to share your story with anyone until you are ready, and even if you begin to share, you may stop at any time.

Week Three

Persistence

Then Jesus told them a parable about their need to pray always and not to lose heart. He said, "In a certain city there was a judge who neither feared God nor had respect for people. In that city there was a widow who kept coming to him and saying, 'Grant me justice against my opponent.' For a while he refused; but later he said to himself, 'Though I have no fear of God and no respect for anyone, yet because this widow keeps bothering me, I will grant her justice, so that she may not wear me out by continually coming.'" And the Lord said, "Listen to what the unjust judge says. And will not God grant justice to his chosen ones who cry to him day and night? Will he delay long in helping them? I tell you, he will quickly grant justice to them."

(Luke 18:1–8)

Reflection: Healing is not an easy journey. There may be days when we want to give up. There may be obstacles that block our path. Sometimes it may seem as though nothing will ever change. Sometimes it seems as though nothing will ever heal our loss. Women who have experienced abuse are like the widow in this story who also experienced a deep loss and a profound injustice. Interestingly, the word *widow* in Hebrew holds the subtlety of meaning of one who is unable to speak.[1] And yet in this story the widow refuses to be silent. She refuses to give up. She knows that her life depends on being able to advocate for herself and her needs. And so she does. It is her persistence against the greatest obstacles that brings her the greatest healing and provides her with the greatest justice. She does not lose heart, and in return, her heart's desire comes true.

What in my life seems like the greatest impediment to my healing? What do I need to persist in doing to help my healing?

(Pause for quiet reflection.)

Prayer: Sustaining God, it often seems as if I will never heal. Each day is a struggle. I wake up and yearn to sleep again. I wake up and wonder how I will survive another day. Today, the biggest obstacle I face is _____ [name the obstacle you face today]. It seems so big and my body trembles when I encounter it. But I know that you have given me a voice to speak up for myself. Give me the courage to face another day. Give me the courage to "pray always and not to lose heart."

Response:

1. As you go to bed, choose a part of your body that helped you persist today and thank that particular part. For example, you may say, "Thank you, feet, for carrying me throughout the day even though you were hurt-

ing," or "Thank you, voice, for speaking up for what I needed even though I was scared."

2. Mark on your calendar or on a piece of paper an event to which you are looking forward this month. Maybe you already have something special planned, such as going to the movies, going to a festival, or celebrating a holiday. Maybe you can plan something special for yourself, such as a long walk on a Sunday morning or a phone call with a friend. Circle the day and let that inspire you to persist.

3. Perhaps there is someone you have been meaning to call but are avoiding. Or maybe there is a form for court or a bill you need to fill out. It is not easy to face the things that intimidate us. Today, promise yourself to do one thing that you have been avoiding. Remember the woman who persistently faced the judge. Receive her courage!

Anger

Then they came to Jerusalem. And he entered the temple and began to drive out those who were selling and those who were buying in the temple, and he overturned tables of the money changers and the seats of those who sold doves; and he would not allow anyone to carry anything through the temple.

(Mark 11:15–16)

Reflection: Jesus loves the temple and does not want people to defile the sacred structure. He becomes angry at the injustice being done against the holy space, and he overturns the "tables of the money changers and the seats of those who sold doves." As Christians, we believe that God resides not only in churches but in our very beings. Our bodies are the temple of God, we are the body of Christ, and the Spirit lives and moves in us. When someone abuses our body, they are defiling our sacred nature. When someone hurts us, they are hurting our holy selves. We should be outraged at the injustice being done to us and, like Jesus, do what we can to stop the violence. We should note, however, that Jesus does not retaliate with violence. He does not hit the money changers and those who sold doves but "overturned tables" and "seats" to keep them from continuing their activity. We, too, must do what we can to overturn the abuse being done to us women individually and collectively. We must not allow anyone to carry on abuse in the holy temple of our lives.

What angers me the most about the abuse I have experienced?

(Pause for quiet reflection.)

Prayer: God, I sometimes forget that you reside within me and how wonderfully I am made. I forget that it is right for me to be angry at any violence done against me. I know that if Jesus were walking the earth he would struggle to protect me. So now let me use my righteous anger at abuse and struggle to protect myself with the Spirit that lives in me. I promise I will try to keep my body safe. I promise I will call upon others if I need help to do so. I promise to honor the holy temple that is my body.

Response:

1. You may not be able to feel any anger yet. Sometimes women who have experienced abuse feel sadness before anger, or numbness before rage. In prayer, tell God how you are feeling. Ask God to be with you as you feel the emotional aftermath of abuse. Ask God to lead you through a range of emotions that will take you through your healing journey.

2. You may feel a lot of anger but not know how to express it. One way to express anger is through safe physical activity or through art. You may try kicking a ball on a field or going for a run. Or try gathering some art supplies that are accessible to you—maybe a pencil, crayons, finger paints, etc.—and let yourself draw whatever you like on a blank page. It doesn't need to be anything recognizable. Let your anger pour onto the page.

3. A way to express anger productively is through working to change the societal structures that perpetuate systems of abuse. For example, you may choose to get involved in an organization that works to help women who experience the injustice of domestic violence or unjust welfare policies. You may find yourself moved to join a peace group that advocates for an end to war and violence. Put your anger to work—see how it is transformed!

Work

A Samaritan woman came to draw water, and Jesus
said to her, "Give me a drink." (His disciples had
gone to the city to buy food.) The Samaritan woman
said to him, "How is it that you, a Jew, ask a drink of
me, a woman of Samaria?" (Jews do not share things
in common with Samaritans.) Jesus answered her,
"If you knew the gift of God, and who it is that is saying to you, 'Give me a drink,' you would have asked
him, and he would have given you living water."
(John 4:7–10)

Reflection: Even though the hurt we have experienced seems
to have put a stop to our lives, in fact our lives continue.
Whether we work in the home or work outside of it, whether
we have a part-time job, a full-time job, or many jobs, or
whether we currently seek employment, we usually must struggle through our healing journey at the same time as we struggle to make a living. The Samaritan woman in this story knows
this dual struggle. She has had five husbands and is probably
ostracized by her community. She is in need of healing but
must continue her work that includes drawing water from the
well. It is in the midst of her daily struggle that Jesus appears
and offers her living water. The water of her well is still, but the
water of which Jesus speaks is not the stagnant water of the well
but a metaphor for a life nourished by the Spirit. As we go
about our work, may we look for wells of living water through-

out our day that might quench our weary bodies. May we ask God to bring us well-being.

Who or what are the "wells" in my life that offer me nourishment?

(Pause for quiet reflection.)

Prayer: Nourishing One, I feel like the Samaritan woman when I am at my job. The abuse I have suffered impedes the work I do. The pain I feel separates me from my colleagues who don't know or fully understand what I have experienced. I thirst for your nourishing presence at work. As I grow weary during the day, come and sit by my side. As I struggle to make a living, give me your living water.

Response:

1. After an experience of abuse, you may find that the things you used to do easily now require more effort. Even getting out of bed and preparing yourself for work may seem impossible. It may feel as though you have nothing to which you may look forward. When you wake in the morning, say to yourself, "I will walk to the well of living water today."

2. As you grow weary with work, it may help to have an inspirational quote or image to calm or uplift you. Find a quote from a newspaper, magazine, poetry book, or novel that inspires you and write it on a slip of paper. Or search through old photos or magazines for a portable image that comforts you. You may even

choose to write your own quote or draw your own image. Then place your creation someplace at work, in a wallet or pocket. Look at it when you are feeling a need for some living water during your day.

3. While you are at work, you may find there are times when you feel overwhelmed. If possible, take a few moments to sit quietly—whether it is in a desk chair, outside on a break, or even in the bathroom. Sit with your back straight and both feet on the floor. If you feel safe, you may choose to close your eyes. Breathe deeply. Imagine that you are drinking from a large jug of clear and nourishing water. Feel it travel down your throat, into your stomach, and throughout your body. It comforts your pain and soothes your nerves. It reawakens you to the day. How does your body feel? Thank God for the living water. When you are ready, open your eyes and go back to your work refreshed.

Generations of Survivors

I am reminded of your sincere faith, a faith that lived first in your grandmother Lois and your mother Eunice and now, I am sure, lives in you....for God did not give us a spirit of cowardice, but rather a spirit of power and of love.

(2 Timothy 1:5, 7)

WOMEN HEALING FROM ABUSE

Reflection: There was a faith in our ancestors that brought them through great suffering, and that faith has been passed along to us. This vigor for life has come to us across the generations, animates our lives, and gives us the courage to face each day. This faith first lived in our foremothers and forefathers and now lives in us.

Who are my ancestors—both familial and cultural—that passed on to me their strength for living? What might they offer me to help me get through this day?

(Pause for quiet reflection.)

Prayer: God, I sometimes feel that I do not have enough faith to open my eyes to the day ahead. I need the faith of my ancestors to support me. Bring me the strength that helped them to survive against the greatest odds. Let me feel their spirits filling me with power to rise today, filling me with love to reach for tomorrow. Guide me as I live in my generation, one strong life in a long line of survivors.

Response:

1. Every woman has a family member—whether born fifty years ago or five hundred years—whose faith gave her the courage to continue to live after she had experienced great suffering. You may not know the name of this ancestor or anything about her, but she understands your suffering. If you feel comfortable, close your eyes. Ask this ancestor to be present to you today. Share with her some of your suffering. Ask her to give

you what you need—her courage, her power, her love, or some other gift of grace.

2. You are a survivor. You have lived through great suffering but you have survived. There was something in you that kept you going. There was a faith within you that wanted to survive. Now you have. Find a place where you feel safe and say the words that you have been living to speak: "I am alive. I have survived. I am part of the generations of survivors." Speak the words as you feel comfortable: whisper them into your pillow, cry them into your hands, sing them into the air.

3. Draw a survivor's family tree. Put people on the tree who have helped you to survive—all the people in your life who have generated life in you, whether immediate family or not. Don't forget to add yourself!

Inner Child

Now when Jesus returned, the crowd welcomed him, for they were all waiting for him. Just then there came a man named Jairus, a leader of the synagogue. He fell at Jesus' feet and begged him to come to his house, for he had an only daughter, about twelve years old, who was dying....

Someone came from the leader's house to say, "Your daughter is dead; do not trouble the teacher any longer." When Jesus heard this, he replied, "Do not fear. Only believe, and she will be saved." When

he came to the house, he did not allow anyone to
enter with him, except Peter, John, and James, and
the child's father and mother. They were all weeping and wailing for her; but he said, "Do not weep;
for she is not dead but sleeping."...He took her by
the hand and called out, "Child, get up!" Her spirit
returned, and she got up at once.

(Luke 8:40–42, 49–52, 54–55)

Reflection: The adults feared that the young girl had died. But
Jesus tells them, "Do not fear. Only believe, and she will be
saved." When we have been abused, it may seem as though our
inner child, that part of ourselves that is vibrant and ready for
the world, has been beaten, bruised, and left for dead. Has our
thirst for life died? Has our curiosity for the world been killed?
Jesus says no. The child we think we have lost inside us "is not
dead but sleeping," and her spirit will return to us. She will
awake and rise again. She will be healed.

Whether abuse occurs to a child or to an adult, violence
always harms one's inner child or inner joy. *What do I want to
say to my inner child? May I ask her to rise today from her long
sleep?*

(Pause for quiet reflection.)

Prayer: Playful God, I find it difficult to find joy in life. I have
no energy within me to face the day. I no longer see the brilliance in the small things of life. I mourn for the inner child
that I fear has passed away. Help me to remember that she is
not dead but sleeping. Help me to remember that my inner joy

simply rests within me and that I may call to her, "Child, get up!" Let my joyous spirit for life return. Let my inner child arise.

Response:

1. Your inner child "is not dead but sleeping." Try waking her today. Gently call to her as you would to waken a sleeping child. Ask her to rise.
2. Put on some music and let yourself dance around the room. Let your inner child, your inner joy, dance freely.
3. To awaken your inner child, try doing something you used to do in your youth. Savor a piece of candy, play a game, or skip down the street. As you smile, know that your inner child is alive and well.

Choice

Then Mary said, "Here am I, the servant of the Lord; let it be with me according to your word."
(Luke 1:38)

Reflection: Women often feel as though they are limited in their ability to make their own decisions in life. We feel these limits even more after an experience of abuse, when the person who hurt us may have restricted our ability to make our own choices. But we *can* make our own decisions. The biblical passage above offers us an example of one woman's courage to choose. Despite the limits placed on women at this point in history, God offers Mary a choice. She chooses to receive God's presence. She says yes to life. By making decisions, she is affirming her independence, her own human capabilities, her own sacred self. She is saying to the world, "Here am I." She is saying, "This is my choice, this is who I am."

What are some decisions I have made that brought me a feeling of new life and joy?

(Pause for quiet reflection.)

Prayer: God, my experience of abuse has left me feeling as if I cannot make decisions. I feel powerless. But then I remember Mary. She, too, was a woman who probably felt frightened at what lay ahead, but she summoned her courage and made a choice. Give me the power to choose, too. Give me the courage to make decisions, not according to what will please others, but according to what will help me to heal. I want to say "yes" to life. I want to say "yes" to the world. I want to tell the world I am still here. Here am I!

Response:

1. Feeling some control of yourself and your life is diffi-cult when so much in your experience has been chaos. It may even seem hard to decide to begin your journey toward healing. Try saying silently or aloud, "I choose to heal."
2. After having been restricted in decision making, you have reason to celebrate when you are able to make

choices again. What choices do you make now that you were not able to make before? Did the person who hurt you limit the type or quantity of food you ate? Decide to cook yourself a favorite dish. Did the person who caused you pain want you to act or dress in a certain way? Choose to act according to what you feel is most appropriate, or put on a pair of your most comfortable clothes. You are free to choose.

3. Make a list of dreams you had as a child—anything from being a teacher to growing flowers. How have your dreams changed? Are any still the same? Is there a dream you still want to pursue? How might you choose to take up that dream again? For example, if you wanted to be a teacher, is there still a way to reach that dream? Perhaps you will choose to take education courses toward your teacher certification or decide to mentor a child through a volunteer program. Or maybe you find that you are already a teacher to your children or to a young family relative in a hundred daily ways. However you choose to pursue your dreams, remember, it is you who gets to decide.

Rediscovering Myself

[Jesus said,] "Or what woman having ten silver coins, if she loses one of them, does not light a lamp, sweep the house, and search carefully until she finds it? When she has found it, she calls together her

friends and neighbors, saying, 'Rejoice with me, for
I have found the coin that I had lost.'" (Luke 15:8–9)

Reflection: When we suffer abuse, it may seem that we have
lost a part of ourselves. If the abuse occurred in our teenage
years or in adulthood, we may have hidden a treasured aspect
of ourselves in order to survive the abuse. If the abuse happened during our childhood, we may have lost the opportunity
to develop an aspect of ourselves had the abuse not occurred.
Now, during the healing journey, we may finally look for that
treasured part of ourselves that we were forced to keep hidden
or undeveloped. We may light the lamp of our hearts and seek
what was lost. We may sweep the memories of our youth for
what we had to give up or we may clean away that which keeps
us from developing into the person we were meant to be. And
when we find that treasured part of ourselves, we shall rejoice!

*What did I treasure about myself before the abuse began?
Or, if the abuse began with the earliest memories I have, what
aspect of myself might I develop that I was unable to develop
before?*

(Pause for quiet reflection.)

Prayer: Gracious God, it feels as if I have lost a part of myself.
I may not even be able to name what it is but I know that I do
not feel complete. I want to find what is lost. I want to feel
whole. I want to discover that part of myself that makes me
happy to be alive. I want to rejoice. Help me to know what is
missing. Help me to search the corners of my heart so that I

may be able to exclaim, like the woman with the lost coin, "Rejoice with me, for I have found the treasure that I had lost!"

Response:

1. Although you may feel as though you have lost a part of yourself, it is still lying within you. It is only dormant. During your prayer time, thank your body for carrying all parts of you during this long journey and for keeping you as whole as possible.

2. Make a list of some things you used to love to do or wish you had been able to do as a child. Perhaps you liked to or wished you could tell jokes or act silly, go out by yourself or with friends, share love or feel loved. Choose one activity from your list and plan how you will do it this week.

3. Using the list you made in the response above, call a friend and do one of the lost activities together.

Week Four

God Changes

> Mary Magdalene went and announced to the disciples, "I have seen the Lord"; and she told them that he had said these things to her. (John 20:18)

Reflection: Mary Magdalene suffered tremendously. First, she suffered from afflictions. Then, she suffered when her beloved Jesus was crucified. Now her world has been turned upside down. Everything she thought she knew about Jesus has been taken from her. But then, in the midst of her mourning, Jesus appears. Jesus comes to her in a new form. Mary comes to understand that God appears in our lives in different ways. She runs to the apostles and says, "I have seen the Lord." As women who have suffered abuse, we have suffered like Mary. Our worlds have been turned upside down. Even our faith may seem lost. But as we heal, we discover that God comes to us in different ways. Some images of God that our faith tradition gave us may no longer resonate with us. Some of the ways in which our faith tradition talks about God may not represent the ways we have come to know God through our times of suffering and healing. But God has appeared to us in a new form and asks us to share this good news.

How did I imagine God as a child? How have I imagined God as an adult? How does God come to me now?

(Pause for quiet reflection.)

Prayer: God of Many Names, as a child I may have imagined you as a strong Father. Now that I have suffered abuse, my images of you may have changed. Sometimes I may still think of you as a parent, but I also think of you as my friend that I run to when I am lonely, my counselor with whom I may speak when I am scared, my healer that I embrace when I feel broken. When the nightmares come, you whisper, "Do not be afraid." When the day overwhelms me, you sing, "Peace be with you." You are the God of the resurrection. You are the God of my transformation. You are the God of healing and change. Truly, I have seen the Lord!

Response:

1. It may be difficult to pray at this time. But God comes to us in different ways. Some find God at church. Others find God in one's neighbors, in one's family, in one's prayers at home. Where do you find God these days? On a walk in the neighborhood? In the garden like Mary Magdalene? At home in your heart?

2. With your new ways of experiencing God, you may want to create your own new religious art. Draw a picture of something that reminds you of God in your midst.

3. Experiencing God in new ways may be unfamiliar at first, but it may also be exciting. You may want to share

your encounters of God with someone as Mary Magdalene did. Is there a friend or a local religious leader with whom you could talk about your experiences? Perhaps they have come to know God in new ways, too.

Friends

In those days Mary set out and went with haste to a Judean town in the hill country, where she entered the house of Zechariah and greeted Elizabeth. When Elizabeth heard Mary's greeting, the child leaped in her womb. And Elizabeth was filled with the Holy Spirit and exclaimed with a loud cry, "Blessed are you among women...." (Luke 1:39–42)

Reflection: When we are abused, we often find ourselves isolated from family and friends. Sometimes our abuser did not like when we spent time with other people. Sometimes we said good-bye to friends because we could not bear to tell them the truth of what was happening. Sometimes we lost our friends because they could not understand the situation we faced. There were even times when we just did not have the energy to pick up the phone and call someone. It is hard now to reconnect with family and friends, but it is also hard to be alone. Mary knew when she needed the company of a friend. She ran to her friend and cousin Elizabeth. Elizabeth greeted Mary and cried out with joy at their meeting. Elizabeth reminded Mary that she was blessed.

Who are my friends? Whom can I turn to for friendship? Who will welcome me with joy as Elizabeth welcomed Mary?

(Pause for quiet reflection.)

Prayer: Companion God, I feel very alone sometimes. It is hard to reach out to friends when I spend all my energy just trying to make it through the day. When Mary needed a friend, you blessed her with Elizabeth. Help me to remember that you are my friend, walking with me each day. Help me to reach out to old and new friends who, like Elizabeth, will remind me that I am blessed and that I am filled with good.

Response:

1. Imagine God sitting at your side. If you feel comfortable, ask God to hold you in a warm embrace and to bless you for the day ahead.
2. Who from your past makes you feel blessed and cared for? Call or write them, thank them for what they have meant to you, and plan to correspond or meet again soon.
3. Is there a church, community center, support meeting, or other environment where you may feel safe interacting with new people? Stay for coffee hour after a church service, sign up for a fun class, or attend a meeting where you may meet new friends.

Love

Upon my bed at night
  I sought him who my soul loves....
I adjure you, O daughters of Jerusalem,
  by the gazelles or the wild does:
do not stir up or awaken love
  until it is ready!

(Song of Solomon 3:1, 5)

Reflection: After we have experienced abuse, it takes a while for our hearts to heal. It may feel as though someone has stolen our heart or taken a piece of it. And yet it is important that we not try to fill that emptiness instantly with something or someone else that will damage our heart: alcohol, drugs, an unhealthy relationship, or some other emptiness-filler. Instead, we must take our time. We must wait until we, like the woman in the Song of Solomon, find the one whom our soul loves, the one who will not abuse us body and soul. We may experience loneliness while we wait, but we may also experience love in new ways—with ourselves, with friends, with beloved pets, with God. We will learn to love ourselves and to experience healthy ways of loving so that we will know if and when we are ready to stir up or awaken a new intimate love.

Can I imagine God's love embracing me for now until I am ready to move on with a new person in my life?

(Pause for quiet reflection.)

Prayer: Loving God, sometimes I still feel love for the person who hurt me, but I know that I cannot love someone who does not fully love me for who I am. And my heart aches. There are times when I feel that I will never love again. There are times when I feel that I will be too scared to love again. For now, I will keep my own company until I want to awaken love with someone else. I will not allow my soul to be beaten again. I will wait for the one whom my soul loves, someone who will love my own soul in return.

Response:

1. After surviving abuse, it may be frightening to even think about entering into a new relationship. That is OK. All you need to do now is to love yourself. You can seek yourself as the one whom your soul loves. As you sit quietly, imagine the parts of yourself that you love: perhaps your legs that carry you through the day, your hands that cook and care for you, or your heart that loves you as you are.

2. You have learned a lot about love in the past. Take out a sheet of paper and write a list of the things you have learned about how to be in relationship with someone else. What characteristics should be or not be in a relationship? What are the qualities that you want or don't want in another person with whom you are in relationship?

3. Perhaps you feel healed enough to enter into a new relationship at this point in your life. How does the person support you and love you for who you are? How do

you communicate with one another? How do you resolve differences? How will this relationship be different? Perhaps at some point in the relationship you will want to discuss these questions with the one whom your soul loves.

Family

So she said, "See, your sister-in-law has gone back to her people and to her gods; return after your sister-in-law." But Ruth said,

"Do not press me to leave you
    or to turn back from following you!
Where you go, I will go;
    where you lodge, I will lodge;
your people shall be my people,
    and your God my God." (Ruth 1:15–16)

Reflection: Ruth's husband dies and her mother-in-law, Naomi, encourages her to return to her own family. However, something about Naomi and her community impels Ruth to stay with her. Her mother-in-law tells her to "return" to her family, but Ruth says she will not "turn back." The biblical writer uses the words *turn, return,* or *go/gone back*—all from the same Hebrew root word—over and over in the first chapter of Ruth. This focus on "turning" reminds us that Ruth has a choice to return to her old family or create a new one. Ruth decides to create a new family for herself with new people and a new way of seeing God. As women who have suffered abuse, we are like Ruth. We have suffered a great loss and we now have the choice to create a new life, a new family. Where shall we turn? Shall we go back to our original families? Shall we return to our old friends? Are there new people in our lives with whom we may create a new family, a new circle of friends—mixing the old with the new? How shall we turn?

Some people have been the cause of great suffering in my life. *Who are the people in my life, from the past or the present, who are the cause of great joy? How may I create new families, new communities with these people?*

(Pause for quiet reflection.)

Prayer: God, you walked with Ruth as she put together a new family. Be with me now as I also re-create my family of friends and loved ones, returning to people from my past and/or turning to people in my present. Give me the courage not to go back to those who refuse to stop hurting me. Give me the strength to go forward to those who love me as I am. Help me to remember that where I go, God, you will go with me. Where I lodge, you will also lodge. Your beloved people will also be my people and you, God, will always be my God. I turn to you.

Response:

1. The most important person as you create a new family is you. Spend a few quiet moments thinking about the roles you have played and contributions you have

made in families—whether biological, foster, or adopted families, or families of friends. What parts of those roles and contributions do you want to keep? What are the parts to which you want to say good-bye?

2. As a child we drew pictures of our families. Take a piece of paper and draw your new family. Who are the people who stand at your side now as you heal?

3. As we create new families for ourselves, they needn't be families as we traditionally think of families. Your new "family" may include a supportive coworker, a kind neighbor, an aunt with whom you reconnect, or the hope of a friend or partner in the future. Is there someone you want to invite or reinvite into your new family?

Intimacy

As they came near the village to which they were going, he walked ahead as if he were going on. But they urged him strongly, saying, "Stay with us, because it is almost evening and the day is now nearly over." So he went in to stay with them. When he was at the table with them, he took bread, blessed and broke it, and gave it to them. Then their eyes were opened, and they recognized him; and he vanished from their sight. They said to each other, "Were not our hearts burning within us while he was talking to us on the road?" (Luke 24:28–32)

Reflection: In the biblical passage, the two companions did not know whom they had invited into their home. But when Jesus broke bread, a symbolic act of love, they were able to discern that this was the friend who loved them and whom they loved. It is common to find that when we invite someone new into our lives, they remind us of someone from our past. As women who have experienced abusive relationships, we may find that new intimate connections trigger memories of former abusive relations. It may be difficult to discern if these memories resurface simply because this is a new relationship or because the new relationship is abusive. We may feel scared. How are we to know if this person will abuse us, too? The story of the road to Emmaus reminds us to look to the new person's actions. Are they actions of love? The story reminds us to listen to our instinct and talk with a companion about our feelings. When we are with someone new, are our hearts burning within us, not with pain, but with deep love?

How does the new person in my life show love to me?

(Pause for quiet reflection.)

Prayer: Loving God, I want to invite someone new into my life but I want to ensure that I will not be hurt again. Help me to discern if this person will love me for who I am. On the road to Emmaus the two companions' "eyes were opened." Open my eyes to see the truth in this relationship. Strengthen my heart so that I may say "yes" to a healthy relationship and "no" to a hurtful one. Walk with me on the road of relationships.

Response:

1. Being intimate with someone may make us feel vulnerable. At times we may find ourselves feeling very scared. During these times, you may decide to communicate your fearful feelings with your partner and ask for support. You may decide to take a break from one another's company or see a counselor together. Whatever you decide, it is important to regain a sense of safety, be it alone, with your partner, or with someone else you trust.

2. You may want to share your experience of abuse with someone new in your life. Do not feel pressured to say everything at once. You may begin by simply stating that you have experienced a difficult relationship in the past. If you do decide to share some of your story, do so only after you feel safe and you trust the person with whom you will speak. You may want to put some boundaries around your conversation, such as asking that your confidante not share your story with anyone else, that she or he wait until you are finished telling your story before speaking, and so forth.

3. Jesus was known to the people on the road to Emmaus in the breaking of the bread. How do you and your new friend express your love for each other? Choose to express your love to your partner through words or actions. Perhaps you may decide to leave a note for him or her in an unexpected place, cook a special meal, or take a walk together. Remember, sometimes

the most ordinary actions, such as breaking bread, have the power to open eyes to love.

Healing Others

Soon afterwards he went on through cities and villages, proclaiming and bringing the good news of the kingdom of God. The twelve were with him, as well as some women who had been cured of evil spirits and infirmities: Mary, called Magdalene, from whom seven demons had gone out…. (Luke 8:1–3)

Reflection: Luke's Gospel says that Mary Magdalene "had been cured of evil spirits and infirmities." In biblical times, this often meant that the person was physically ill or emotionally wounded. It is likely that the person experienced a great amount of abuse, not just from their particular ailment, but also from the society that shunned those who were hurting. The fact that Mary suffered from "seven demons" tells us that she probably experienced severe trauma; however, Mary heals from her experience. Now she wants to share her experience of healing with others, to encourage them to stay on the path of healing, however difficult it may seem. She joins Jesus and others who spend their time speaking about and acting for the healing of those who are wounded.

What has helped me most during my healing? If I want to share with others what I have learned from my own experience, how may I do that?

WOMEN HEALING FROM ABUSE

(Pause for quiet reflection.)

Prayer: Wise and Just God, I have suffered for so long but I feel myself heal a little more each day. I also know that I am not alone in my struggle to heal. There are millions of other women and men across the world that have suffered, too. Help me to know how I might use the healing and strength I've gained to help myself and others journey through this life with more compassion and joy.

Response:

1. Reflect on your experience of healing. For how many days, months, or years have you been aware of your healing journey? Who has helped you along the way? What experiences helped you heal the most? What hidden strengths have you learned about yourself?

2. Think about the insights and strengths you have discovered about yourself during your healing journey. How may you celebrate those gifts? How may you share those gifts?

3. Think of creative ways for you to share your experience and gifts with others. You may decide to share your experience by talking with your children, nieces or nephews, or other young people about how important it is to be in a relationship of healthy communication and no physical violence. You may decide to share your gift of valuing honesty by speaking the truth in a particular situation. Discover your mission.

Community

Now there was a woman who had been suffering from hemorrhages for twelve years; and though she had spent all she had on physicians, no one could cure her. She came up behind him and touched the fringe of his clothes, and immediately her hemorrhage stopped. Then Jesus asked, "Who touched me?" When all denied it, Peter said, "Master, the crowds surround you and press in on you." But Jesus said, "Someone touched me; for I noticed that power had gone out from me." When the woman saw that she could not remain hidden, she came trembling; and falling down before him, she declared in the presence of all the people why she had touched him, and how she had been immediately healed. He said to her, "Daughter, your faith has made you well; go in peace." (Luke 8:43–48)

Reflection: You have suffered for years in pain—physical, emotional, and spiritual. As a result of the trauma, you may feel isolated from others in your pain. You may feel that you have sought help but have not found healing. The woman in this biblical passage has also suffered. The woman in this passage has also reached out for help but received nothing in return. Today, she courageously reaches out for help one more time. By reaching for the "fringe of his clothes," she not only touches Jesus, but also touches the fringe of his Jewish prayer shawl. She is not only reaching out for physical healing, but she is reaching out to her spiritual community—her faith—with the hope of feeling whole again. And to her astonishment, her pain subsides. But Jesus calls out, "Who touched me?" He knows that her physical healing is only part of her recovery process and that she will heal more fully when she makes a healing, healthy connection with another human and feels part of the community again. She comes forward, despite her fears, and finds welcomed safety in the crowd, boldly shares her story, and reconnects with her community. Through her own actions, her faith, and the assistance of the community, she moves through the stages of healing and into a sense of communion and commonality with others. She moves from the margins of society to a sense of belonging. She moves from the fringe to fullness of life.

Who is my community or what type of community am I looking for?

(Pause for quiet reflection.)

Prayer: Healing God, the woman of this scripture passage suffered for twelve years, but I know how suffering is incalculable. I know how suffering strips you of any sense of time. And the amount of time I have lost to my pain is more than I can bear. But now I am keenly aware of the time left in my life. I am aware I want to start living my life fully. Give me courage to reach out my arms like the woman in this Gospel. Give me the audacity to believe that my faith—in myself, others, you—will heal me. Let me pick up my trembling body and join in the communion of life. May I know my community and myself again. May I go in peace.

Response:

1. It may have been a long time since you have felt part of a community like a family, a neighborhood, a workplace, a town or city, or the larger world. Take a few moments to close your eyes and imagine this scene: You are a child again. An adult that you love and trust takes you to a familiar place from your childhood where there are people. Perhaps it is a town square or a public library. Maybe it is a place of worship or a street in a shopping center. Think of a safe place in that scene where you will not be interrupted but may stand on the side and watch. Imagine the adult kneeling down and holding you as a child in a warm embrace of protection and care. The adult says, "There may be people or things here that scare you but I will protect you. You are part of this community." How does that feel? Then listen. Does the adult say anything else to you? Does the child say anything to the adult? Let those words of safety settle in your heart. When you are ready, open your eyes.

2. Take a piece of paper and draw some circles. In those circles write or draw the names or images of communities that you recall from your past. Did you have a circle of family or friends? Did you have a religious community? Did you take part in a hobby group or a justice/volunteer organization? Did you feel part of the town, city, or country where you lived? Have some of those circles broken apart? What circles do you wish to renew or replace?

3. Think of a community to which you belong; for example, a circle of family or friends, neighbors, coworkers, faith fellowship, city. Chose one and spend thirty minutes there today. Be creative. Perhaps you will stop by a friend's home after work, go for a walk in your neighborhood and say hello to the people you pass, drop by the church and say a prayer, or take a bus to your favorite park. Enjoy being one member of this large community of life here on earth.

Benediction

The meditations have come to an end, but the journey continues. You may always return to these pages as often as you wish. I pray that this book has been and will continue to be a compass on your path, helping you to walk the healing journey. May you always go in peace.

Appendix

Selected Healing Resources

If you choose to access the following information through a computer and you are currently in an abusive relationship, you should be aware that every website you visit leaves a "track" on your computer that can be traced. So you may want to hide your Internet tracks from the person who is abusing you. The safest way to access the Internet is through a public computer at a community center, library, or friend's house. From there, you may also check for other ways to hide your Internet tracks at www.safehorizon.org/page.php?nav=fp&page=warning.

National Domestic Violence Hotline (24 hours a day)
1-800-799-SAFE (7233) or 1-800-787-3224 (TTY)

Counseling
If you decide to seek counseling, ask for a counselor who has training in the area that fits your experience; i.e., child abuse, partner abuse, rape, etc. Also, if you seek a counselor and are currently in an abusive relationship, insist on seeing the counselor individually. Sometimes people who abuse others will use couple or family counseling in unhealthy ways to keep you from leaving the relationship.

WOMEN HEALING FROM ABUSE

American Mental Health Counselors Association
www.amhca.org
801 N. Fairfax St., Ste. 304
Alexandria, VA 22314
800-326-2642

American Psychological Association
www.apa.org
750 First St. NE
Washington, DC 20002-4242
800-374-2721/TDD/TTY: 202-336-6123

National Association of Social Workers
www.naswdc.org
750 First St. NE, Ste. 700
Washington, DC 20002-4241
202-408-8600

Pastoral Counseling
American Association of Pastoral Counselors
http://www.aapc.org/centers.htm
9504A Lee Hwy.
Fairfax, VA 22031-2303
Phone: 703-385-6967
FAX: 703-352-7725
E-Mail: info@aapc.org

National Organizations
FaithTrust Institute
www.faithtrustinstitute.org

2400 N. 45th St. #10
Seattle, WA 98103
206-634-1903

Family Violence Prevention Fund
http://endabuse.org
383 Rhode Island St. Ste. 304
San Francisco, CA 94103
415-252-8900

INCITE! Women of Color Against Violence
www.incite-national.org/about/index.html

National Coalition Against Domestic Violence
www.ncadv.org
NCADV
PO Box 18749
Denver, CO 80218
303-839-1852

National Domestic Violence Hotline
www.hdvh.org

National Network to End Domestic Violence
www.nnedv.org
660 Pennsylvania Ave SE, Ste. 303
Washington, DC 20003
202-543-5566

WOMEN HEALING FROM ABUSE

National Online Resource Center on Violence Against Women
www.vawnet.org
6400 Flank Dr., Ste. 1300
Harrisburg, PA 17112
717-545-6400

The Office on Violence Against Women, US Dept. of Justice
www.usdoj.gov/domesticviolence.htm
800 K St. NW, Ste. 920
Washington, DC 20530
202-307-6026

Rape, Abuse and Incest National Network
www.rainn.org
635-B Pennsylvania Ave. SE
Washington, DC 20003
202-544-1034

Retreat Centers
You may decide that a retreat will help you to focus on your healing or will give you a break from an intensive period of healing. Check these websites for a listing of retreats in your area. Ask if they have programs specifically for healing.
    www.findthedivine.com
    www.retreatfinder.com

Books about Abuse
There are a variety of books on abuse and healing. I recommend searching for books online—again, on a "safe" computer—or at your local library. Your local church or diocese or local domes-

tic violence organization may also be a good source of suggestions. You may search for books on domestic violence in general
or search for a more specific topic, such as abuse and lesbian
relationships, abuse and women of color, or recovery from emotional abuse. To begin, here are two good comprehensive works:

Herman, Judith, MD, *Trauma and Recovery: The Aftermath of
Violence—From Domestic Abuse to Political Terror.* New
York: Basic Books, 1997.
Walker, Lenore E. *The Battered Woman.* HarperCollins: New
York, 1979.

Books about Healing
For further titles you may wish to search online or at your local
library, or ask for suggestions at your parish or diocese or from
a domestic violence organization. Here are some helpful books
to start with:

Adams, Carol J., Marie M. Fortune, et. al. *Violence Against
Women and Children: A Christian Theological Sourcebook.*
New York: Continuum, 1995.
Bass, Ellen, and Laura Davis. *Courage to Heal: A Guide for
Women Survivors of Child Sexual Abuse.* New York:
HarperCollins, 1994.
Benvenga, Nancy. *Healing the Wounds of Emotional Abuse:
The Journey Worth the Risk.* Mineola, NY: Resurrection
Press, 1996.
Brock, Rita Nakashima, and Rebecca Ann Parker, *Proverbs of
Ashes: Violence, Redemptive Suffering, and the Search for
What Saves Us.* Boston: Beacon Press, 2002.

WOMEN HEALING FROM ABUSE

Engel, Beverly. *Breaking the Cycle of Abuse: How to Move Beyond Your Past to Create an Abuse-Free Future.* Hoboken, NJ: John Wiley and Sons, 2005.

Farley, Wendy. *The Wounding and Healing of Desire: Weaving Heaven and Earth.* Louisville, KY: Westminster/John Knox Press, 2005.

Fortune, Marie. *Keeping the Faith: Guidance for Christian Women Facing Abuse.* San Francisco: HarperCollins, 1987.

Jones, Ann. *Next Time She'll Be Dead: Battering and How to Stop It.* Boston: Beacon Press, 1994.

Kaufer, Nelly, and Carol Newhouse-Osmer, *A Woman's Guide to Spiritual Renewal.* San Francisco: HarperSanFrancisco, 1994.

Schüssler Fiorenza, Elisabeth, and Mary Shawn Copeland, eds. *Violence Against Women.* Vol. 1. Maryknoll, NY: Concilium/Orbis Books, 1994.

Smith, Judith R. *Time to Fly Free: Meditations for Those Who Have Left an Abusive Relationship.* Center City, MN: Hazelden, 2001.

Notes

Introduction

1. Judith Herman, MD, *Trauma and Recovery: The Aftermath of Violence — From Domestic Abuse to Political Terror* (New York: Basic Books, 1997), 155.
2. Ibid., 155–74.
3. Catherine Clark Kroeger, "Let's Look Again at the Biblical Concept of Submission," in *Violence Against Women and Children: A Christian Theological Sourcebook*, eds. Carol J. Adams and Marie M. Fortune (New York: Continuum, 1995), 135. In the same book, see Joanne Carlson Brown and Rebecca Parker, "For God so Loved the World?," 37.
4. Marie M. Fortune, "The Transformation of Suffering: A Biblical and Theological Perspective," in *Violence Against Women and Children*, 86.
5. Ibid., 91.
6. Herman, *Trauma and Recovery* 175–95.
7. Ibid., 181.
8. Ibid., 196–213
9. Ibid., 207–11.

Week One

1. Some of these suggestions were shared with me by Nancy Nienhuis, the religion and violence workshop leader at Harvard Divinity School, and dean of students at Andover Newton Theological School.

2. This affirmation was shared with me by Christine Sommers, LICSW.

3. This healing exercise was introduced to me by Vicki Kirsch, LICSW, PhD.

4. While ministering in a parish, I met a man one Sunday who shared with me his struggles with depression and suicide. His counselor had told him that he needed to learn to see beauty in even the grayest of days, even beauty in the shades of gray of an impenetrable, cloudy sky. May we all be able to see God's revelations of beauty on the grayest days of our lives.

Week Two

1. I was introduced to this healing exercise by the Mercy Center in Colorado Springs, CO.

Week Three

1. Jean Broberg Holzapfel and Richard Neitzel Holzapfel, *Sisters at the Well: Women and the Life and Teachings of Jesus* (Salt Lake City, UT: Bookcraft, 1993) 64.